Scottish Police Tests
NUMBERS

www.How2Become.com

by How2become

Attend a 1 Day Police Officer Training Course by visiting:

www.PoliceCourse.co.uk

Get more products for passing Scottish Police selection at:

www.how2become.com

Orders: Please contact How2become Ltd, Suite 14, 50 Churchill Square Business Centre, Kings Hill, Kent ME19 4YU. You can also order via the email address info@how2become.co.uk

ISBN: 978-1910202104

First published in 2014 by How2Become Ltd

Copyright © 2016 How2become.

Typeset for How2become Ltd by Anton Pshinka.

Printed in Great Britain for How2become Ltd by Bell & Bain Ltd, 303 Burnfield Road, Thornliebank, Glasgow G46 7UQ.

CONTENT

As part of this product you have received FREE access to online tests that will help you to pass the Scottish Police Tests!

To gain access, simply go to:

www.PsychometricTestsOnline.co.uk

INTRODUCTION TO YOUR NEW GUIDE

Welcome to Scottish Police Numbers Tests: The ULTIMATE guide for helping you to pass the standard entrance test, for the Scottish Police service. This guide has been designed to help you prepare for, and pass the tough police officer selection process.

The selection process to join the police is highly competitive. Approximately 65,000 people apply to join the police every year. But what is even more staggering is that only approximately 7,000 of those applicants will be successful. You could view this as a worrying statistic, or alternatively you could view it that you are determined to be one of the 7,000 who are successful. Armed with this insider's guide, you have certainly taken the first step to passing the police officer selection process. There are plenty of test questions for you to try out within this guide which are relevant to the NUMBERS test element of the selection process. Once you have completed the testing booklet you may wish to access our online police testing facility which you can find at:

www.how2become.com

Don't ever give up on your dreams; if you really want to become a police officer, then you can do it. The way to approach the police officer selection process is to embark on a programme of 'in-depth' preparation and this guide will help you to do exactly that. The police officer selection process is not easy to pass. Unless, that is, you put in plenty of preparation. Your preparation must be focused in the right areas, and also be comprehensive enough to give you every chance of success. This guide will teach you how to be a successful candidate.

The way to pass the police officer selection process is to develop your own skills and experiences around the core competencies that are required to become a police officer. Many candidates who apply to join the police will be unaware that the core competencies even exist. This guide has been specifically designed to help you prepare for the Police Initial Recruitment Test that forms part of the assessment centre.

About the Scottish Police Standard Entrance Test

The test is made up of three papers. There are three different versions of the test, therefore all applicants are allowed to sit the Standard Entrance Test (SET) a maximum of three times. The test covers:

- language
- numbers
- information handling

To help you get ready for the test, we've created sample NUMBERS test questions for you to practice. Work through each test carefully before checking your answers at the end of the test. If you need any further help with any element of the police officer selection process, including role play, written test and interview, then we offer a wide range of products to assist you. These are all available through our online shop **www.how2become.com.** We also run a 1-day intensive Police Officer Course.

Details are available at the website:

www.PoliceCourse.co.uk

Once again, thank you for your custom and we wish you every success in your pursuit to becoming a police officer.

Work hard, stay focused and be what you want...

Best wishes,

The How2become Team

100 WARM-UP QUESTIONS

Get FREE access to more tests at:

www.PsychometricTestsOnline.co.uk

100 WARM-UP QUESTIONS

Within this first test there are 100 sample warm-up questions to get you prepared for the test exercises that follow. There is no time limit for this particular test; however, it is important that you work through all of the questions as quickly as possible without the aid of a calculator.

1. 18 + 26

Answer [   ]

2. 97 - 46

Answer [   ]

3. 12 x 64

Answer [   ]

4. 5 x (12 x 11)

Answer [   ]

5. 74 / 4

Answer [   ]

6. 4 x (4 + 5)

Answer [   ]

7. 11 x (4 + 5)

Answer [   ]

8. 80 / 5

Answer [   ]

9. 4 x 4 x 6

Answer [   ]

10. 8 x (8 - 6)

Answer [   ]

11. 12 / 4 x 6

Answer [   ]

12. 100 / (4 + 1)

Answer [   ]

13. 216 – 158

Answer [   ]

14. 196 + 658

Answer [   ]

15. 856 / 2

Answer [   ]

16. (4 x 4) + (5 x 6)

Answer [   ]

17. (4 + 6) x (12 − 6)

Answer [   ]

18. 30 / 2 / 3

Answer [   ]

19. 2 x 3 x 4

Answer [   ]

20. 146 / 2

Answer [   ]

21. 123 x 3

Answer [   ]

22. 72 / (8 + 10)

Answer [   ]

23. 1234 x 4

Answer [   ]

24. 453 + 1987

Answer [   ]

25. 45 x 46

Answer [   ]

26. 182 + 4 x 2

Answer [   ]

27. 9753 – 679

Answer [   ]

28. 7547 − 975

Answer [ ]

29. 380 x 60

Answer [ ]

30. (6 x 12) x (8 x 15)

Answer [ ]

31. 12 x 123

Answer [ ]

32. 5589 + 3797

Answer [ ]

33. 35 x 235 − 17

Answer [ ]

34. (36 / 3) + 58

Answer [ ]

35. 864 x 468

Answer [   ]

36. 985 / 5

Answer [   ]

37. (78 / 2) x 13

Answer [   ]

38. (46 x 12) x 4

Answer [   ]

39. 4 x (108 – 76)

Answer [   ]

40. (45 + 75) – 14

Answer [   ]

41. (49 – 38) x (13 + 12)

Answer [   ]

42. 690 / 5 x 2

Answer [ ]

43. 876 / 2 + 4

Answer [ ]

44. 76 x 97

Answer [ ]

45. 863 x 10

Answer [ ]

46. 9856 – 8753

Answer [ ]

47. 7854 – 975

Answer [ ]

48. 2 x (6035 + 204)

Answer [ ]

49. 58 x 29

Answer [   ]

50. 12 x (4 + 6)

Answer [   ]

51. (873 – 3) – (456 – 123)

Answer [   ]

52. 30 x (150 / 10)

Answer [   ]

53. (120 x 12) – (10 x 2)

Answer [   ]

54. 2435 + 38

Answer [   ]

55. 9786 – 134

Answer [   ]

56. 2804 – 2467

Answer [   ]

57. 60 x (4 x 4)

Answer [   ]

58. (9 x 8) / 12

Answer [   ]

59. 2 x (6 x 12) + 3 x (4 + 7)

Answer [   ]

60. 986 / 2

Answer [   ]

61. 23 x (57 + 93)

Answer [   ]

62. 12 x 5 x 6

Answer [   ]

63. 4793 – 1037 + 837

Answer [   ]

64. (10 x 6) / 3

Answer [   ]

65. 8276 – 1256

Answer [   ]

66. 8463 + 2480

Answer [   ]

67. 8436 – 8406 / 2

Answer [   ]

68. 349 x 87

Answer [   ]

69. 984 / 6

Answer [   ]

70. 2379 + 238

Answer [   ]

71. 12 x (502 + 38)

Answer [   ]

72. 39 x (93 - 87)

Answer [   ]

73. 3498 – 2002

Answer [   ]

74. (19 x 38) + (13 x 4)

Answer [   ]

75. 58 x 3

Answer [   ]

76. 974 x 4

Answer [   ]

77. 840 / 4

Answer

78. 431 x 30

Answer

79. 34 x 97

Answer

80. 984 – 94

Answer

81. (83 - 71) + (38 x 3)

Answer

82. 2379 – 100 + 345

Answer

83. 2 x (50 x 4) + 4 x (4 - 2)

Answer

84. 34 − 30 x 6

Answer [ ]

85. 23 x (90 / 5)

Answer [ ]

86. 8916 + 9383

Answer [ ]

87. 120 x 432

Answer [ ]

88. 900 / 12

Answer [ ]

89. (23 x 6) − (12 - 3)

Answer [ ]

90. 124 − 93

Answer [ ]

91. 973 + 804

Answer [ ]

92. 2 x (83 + 27) + 3 x (5 x 6)

Answer [ ]

93. 8542 – 1267

Answer [ ]

94. 36 / (12 - 6)

Answer [ ]

95. 40 / (5 x 2)

Answer [ ]

96. 235 x 125

Answer [ ]

97. 884 / 4

Answer [ ]

98. 2367 x 23

Answer [   ]

99. 64 x 34

Answer [   ]

100. (23 x 34) + (34 x 12)

Answer [   ]

ANSWERS TO 100 WARM-UP QUESTIONS

1. 44
2. 51
3. 768
4. 660
5. 18.5
6. 36
7. 99
8. 16
9. 96
10. 16
11. 18
12. 20
13. 58

14. 854

15. 428

16. 46

17. 60

18. 5

19. 24

20. 73

21. 369

22. 4

23. 4936

24. 2440

25. 2070

26. 190

27. 9074

28. 6572

29. 22800

30. 8640

31. 1476

32. 9386

33. 8208

34. 70

35. 404352

36. 197

37. 507

38. 2208

39. 128

40. 106

41. 275

42. 276

43. 442

44. 7372

45. 8630

46. 1103

47. 6879

48. 12478

49. 1682

50. 120

51. 537

52. 450

53. 1420

54. 2473

55. 9652

56. 337

57. 960

58. 6

59. 177

60. 493

61. 3450

62. 360

63. 2919

64. 20

65. 7020

66. 10943

67. 4233

68. 30363

69. 164

70. 2617

71. 6480

72. 234

73. 1496

74. 774

75. 174

76. 3896

77. 210

78. 12930

79. 3298

80. 890

81. 126

82. 1934

83. 408

84. -146

85. 414

86. 18299

87. 51840

88. 75

89. 129

90. 31

91. 1777

92. 310

93. 7275

94. 6

95. 4

96. 29375

97. 221

98. 54441

99. 2176

100. 1190

Congratulations on completing the warm-up questions. Now move onto the timed numbers exercises contained within the remainder of your guide.

NUMBERS EXERCISE 1

Get FREE access to more tests at:

www.PsychometricTestsOnline.co.uk

NUMBERS EXERCISE 1

Try to answer the questions quickly and without the use of a calculator. You have 5 minutes in which to answer the 14 questions.

1. A wallet has been found containing one £20 note, five £5 notes, a fifty pence coin and three 2 pence coins. How much is in the wallet?

Answer [   ]

2. Subtract 200 from 500, add 80, subtract 30 and multiply by 2. What number do you have?

Answer [   ]

3. A multi-storey car park has 8 floors and can hold 72 cars on each floor. In addition to this, there are 4 allocated disable parking spaces per floor. How many spaces are there in the entire car park?

Answer [   ]

4. A man saves £12.50 per month. How much would he have saved after 1 year?

Answer [   ]

5. If there has been 60 accidents along one stretch of a motorway in the last year, how many on average have occurred each month?

Answer [   ]

6. Out of 40,000 applicants only 4,000 are likely to be successful. What percentage will fail?

Answer [   ]

7. What percentage of 400 is 100?

Answer [   ]

8. Malcolm's shift commences at 0615 hours. If his shift is 10.5 hours long what time will he finish?

Answer [   ]

9. If Mary can bake 12 cakes in 2 hours, how many will she bake in 10 hours?

Answer [   ]

10. If there are 24 hours in the day, how many hours are there in one week?

Answer [   ]

11. Susan has 10 coins and gives 5 of them to Steven and the remainder to Alan. Alan gives 3 of his coins to Steven who in turn gives half of his back to Susan. How many is Susan left with?

Answer [   ]

12. Add 121 to 54. Now subtract 75 and multiply by 10. What is the result?

Answer [   ]

13. Ahmed leaves for work at 8am and arrives at work at 9.17am. He then leaves work at 4.57pm and arrives back at home at 6.03pm. How many minutes has Ahmed spent travelling?

Answer [   ]

14. A car travels at 30 km/h for the first hour, 65km/h for the second hour, 44 km/h for the third hour and 50 km/h for the fourth hour. What is the car's average speed over the 4-hour journey?

Answer [   ]

ANSWERS TO NUMBERS EXERCISE 1

For this section, we have provided you detailed explanations to show you how to work out the answers.

1. £45.56

20.00 + 5.00 + 5.00 + 5.00 + 5.00 + 5.00 + 0.50 + 0.06 = £45.56

2. 700

500 − 200 = 300

300 + 80 − 30 = 350 x 2 = 700

3. 608

(8 x 72) + (4 x 8) = 576 + 32 = 608

4. £150

12.50 x 12 = £150

5. 5

60 ÷ 12 = 5

6. 90%

Out of 40,000 applicants, 36,000 people will fail. 10% of 40,000 = 4,000.

36,000 ÷ 4,000 = 9% x 10 = 90% of people will fail.

7. 25%

100 is 25% of 400.

8. 1645 hours or 4.45pm

You need to add 10 hours and 30 minutes to 0615 which gives you the answer of 4.45 pm.

9. 60 cakes

If Mary can bake 12 cakes in 2 hours, in 10 hours, she will be able to make 60.

12 x 5 = 60

10. 168

24 x 7 = 168 hours

11. 4

Susan has 10 coins and gives 5 to Stephen – Stephen now has 5. She gives the remainder to Alan, so now Alan has 5, but he gives three of them to Stephen – Stephen now has 8. He gives half of them back to Susan, so Susan now has 4.

12. 1000

121 + 54 = 175

175 – 75 = 100 x 10 = 1000

13. 143 minutes

8 am to 9.17 am = 1 hour and 17 minutes (77 minutes)

4.57 pm to 6:03 pm = 1 hour and 6 minutes (66 minutes)

77 + 66 = 143 minutes

14. 47.25 km/h

30 + 65 + 44 + 50 = 189

189 divided by 4 hours = 47.25

NUMBERS EXERCISE 2

Get FREE access to more tests at:

www.PsychometricTestsOnline.co.uk

NUMBERS EXERCISE 2

You are not permitted to use a calculator during this exercise.
You have 10 minutes in which to answer 20 multiple-choice questions.

1. Your friends tell you their electricity bill has gone up from £40 per month to £47 per month. How much extra are they now paying per year?

a. £84 b. £85 c. £83 d. £86 e. £82

Answer [   ]

2. A woman earns a salary of £32,000 per year. How much would she earn in 15 years?

a. £280,000 b. £380,000 c. £480,000 d. £260,000 e. £460,000

Answer [   ]

3. If a police officer walks the beat for 6 hours at a pace of 4km/h, how much ground will she have covered after the 6 hours is over?

a. 20km b. 21km c. 22km d. 23km e. 24km

Answer [   ]

4. It takes Malcolm 45 minutes to walk 6 miles to work. At what pace does he walk?

a. 7 mph b. 4 mph c. 6 mph d. 5 mph e. 8 mph

Answer [   ]

5. Ellie spends 3 hours on the phone talking to her friend abroad. If the call costs 12 pence per 5 minutes, how much does the call cost in total?

a. £3.30 b. £4.32 c. £3.32 d. £4.44 e. £3.44

Answer [   ]

6. A woman spends £27 in a retail store. She has a discount voucher that reduces the total cost to £21.60. How much discount does the voucher give her?

a. 5%   b. 10%   c. 15%   d. 20%   e. 25%

Answer [   ]

7. A group of 7 men spend £21.70 on a round of drinks. How much does each of them pay if the bill is split evenly?

a. £3.00   b. £65.10   c. £3.10   d. £3.15   e. £3.20

Answer [   ]

8. 45,600 people attend a football match to watch Manchester United play Tottenham Hotspur. If there are 32,705 Manchester United supporters at the game, how many Tottenham Hotspur supporters are there?

a. 12,985   b. 13,985   c. 12,765   d. 12,895   e. 14,985

Answer [   ]

9. The police are called to attend a motorway accident involving a coach full of passengers. A total of 54 people are on board, 17 of whom are injured. How many are not injured?

a. 40   b. 39   c. 38   d. 37   e. 36

Answer [   ]

10. A car journey usually takes 6 hrs and 55 minutes, but on one occasion, the car also has to stop for an extra 47 minutes. How long does the journey take on this occasion?

a. 6 hrs 40 mins   b. 5 hrs 45 mins   c. 7 hrs 40 mins   d. 7 hrs 42 mins

e. 6 hrs 42 mins

Answer

11. There are 10 people in a team. Five of them weigh 70 kg each and the remaining 5 weigh 75 kg each. What is the average weight of the team?

a. 72.5 kg   b. 71.5 kg   c. 70.5 kg   d. 72 kg   e. 71 kg

Answer

12. A kitchen floor takes 80 tiles to cover. A man buys 10 boxes, each containing 6 tiles. How many more boxes does he need to complete the job?

a. 2 boxes   b. 4 boxes   c. 6 boxes   d. 8 boxes   e. 10 boxes

Answer

13. How much money does it cost to buy 12 packets of crisps at 47 pence each?

a. £6.45   b. £5.64   c. £6.54   d. £4.65   e. £5.46

Answer

14. A motorcyclist is travelling at 78 mph on a road where the speed limit is 50 mph. How much over the speed limit is he?

a. 20 mph   b. 22 mph   c. 26 mph   d. 28 mph   e. 30 mph

Answer

15. A removal firm loads 34 boxes onto a van. If there are 27 boxes still to be loaded, how many boxes are there in total?

a. 49   b. 50   c. 61   d. 52   e. 53

Answer

16. When paying a bill at the bank you give the cashier one £20 note, two £5 notes, four £1 coins, six 10p coins and two 2p coins. How much have you given him?

a. £34.64   b. £43.46   c. £34.46   d. £63.44   e. £36.46

Answer

17. If you pay £97.70 per month on your council tax bill, how much would you pay quarterly?

a. £293.30   b. £293.20   c. £293.10   d. £293.00   e. £292.90

Answer

18. Four people eat a meal at a restaurant. The total bill comes to £44.80. How much do they need to pay each?

a. £10.00   b. £10.10   c. £10.20   d. £11.10   e. £11.20

Answer

19. A worker is required to work for 8 hours a day. He is entitled to three 20-minute breaks and one 1-hour lunch break during that 8-hour period. If he works for 5 days per week, how many hours will he have worked after 4 weeks?

a. 12 hours b. 14 hours c. 120 hours d. 140 hours e. 150 hours

Answer [   ]

20. If there are 610 metres in a mile, how many metres are there in 4 miles?

a. 240   b. 2040   c. 2044   d. 2440   e. 244

Answer [   ]

ANSWERS TO NUMBERS EXERCISE 2

For this section, we have provided you detailed explanations to show you how to work out the answers.

1. a. £84

In this question you need to first work out the difference in their electricity bill. Subtract £40 from £47 to be left with £7. Now you need to calculate how much extra they are paying per year. If there are 12 months in a year then you need to multiply £7 by 12 months to reach your answer of £84.

2. c. £480,000

The lady earns £32,000 per year. To work out how much she earns in 15 years, you must multiply £32,000 by 15 years to reach your answer of £480,000.

3. e. 24km

To work this answer out all you need to do is multiply the 6 hours by the 4 km/h to reach the total of 24 km. Remember that she is walking at a pace of 4 km per hour for a total of 6 hours.

4. e. 8mph

Malcolm walks 6 miles in 45 minutes, which means he is walking two miles every 15 minutes. Therefore, he would walk 8 miles in 60 minutes (1 hour), so he is walking at 8 mph.

5. b. £4.32

If the call costs 12 pence for every 5 minutes, then all you need to do is cal-culate how many 5 minutes there are in the 3-hour telephone call. There are 60 minutes in every hour, so therefore there are 180 minutes in 3 hours. 180 minutes divided by 5 minutes will give you 36. To get your answer, just multiply 36 by 12 pence to reach your answer of £4.32

6. d. 20%

This type of question can be tricky, especially when you don't have a calcula-tor! The best way to work out the answer is to first of all work out how much 10% discount would give you off the total price. If £27 is the total price, then 10% would be a £2.70 discount. In monetary terms, the woman has received £5.40 in discount. If 10% is a £2.70 discount, then 20% is a £5.40 discount.

7. c. £3.10

Divide £21.70 by 7 to reach your answer of £3.10.

8. d. 12,895

Subtract 32,705 from 45,600 to reach your answer of 12,895.

9. d. 37

Subtract 17 from 54 to reach your answer of 37.

10. d. 7 hrs 42 minutes

Add the 47 minutes to the normal journey time of 6 hrs and 55 minutes to reach your answer of 7 hrs and 42 minutes.

11. a. 72.5 kg

To calculate the average weight, you need to first of all add each weight together. Therefore, (5 x 70) + (5 x 75) = 725 kg. To find the average weight you must now divide the 725 by 10, which will give you the answer 72.5 kg.

12. b. 4 boxes

The man has 10 boxes, each of which contains 6 tiles. He therefore has a total of 60 tiles. He now needs a further 20 tiles to cover the total floor area. If there are 6 tiles in a box, then he will need a further 4 boxes (24 tiles).

13. b. £5.64

Multiply 12 by 47 pence to reach your answer of £5.64.

14. d. 28 mph

Subtract 50 mph from 78 mph to reach your answer of 28 mph.

15. c. 61

Add 34 to 27 to reach your answer of 61 boxes.

16. a. £34.64

Add all of the money together to reach the answer of £34.64.

17. c. £293.10

To reach the answer you must multiply £97.70 by 3. Remember, a quarter is every 3 months.

18. e. £11.20

Divide £44.80 by 4 people to reach your answer of £11.20.

19. c. 120 hours

First of all you need to determine how many 'real' hours he works each day. Subtract the total sum of breaks from 8 hours to reach 6 hours per day. If he works 5 days per week, then he is working a total of 30 hours per week. Multiply 30 hours by 4 weeks to reach your answer of 120 hours.

20. d. 2440 metres

Multiply 4 by 610 metres to reach your answer of 2440 metres.

NUMBERS EXERCISE 3

Get FREE access to more tests at:

www.PsychometricTestsOnline.co.uk

NUMBERS EXERCISE 3

Try to answer the questions quickly and without the use of a calculator. You have 12 minutes in which to answer the 25 questions.

1. A rugby stadium holds 36,000 spectators. The ratio of police to spectators is to be 1:180. How many police officers will be needed?

Answer [   ]

2. Heavy winds during the week resulted in the suspension bridge being closed between the hours of 1345 and 1630 on Tuesday, 1005 and 1150 on Thursday and 0800 and 1015 on Friday. For how long (in hours and minutes) was the bridge closed altogether?

Answer [   ]

3. There are 4 squares, 1 circle and 3 rectangles on a page. How many 90 degree angles are there?

Answer [   ]

4. Sally parked her car at 13:00pm. The car park allows for 2 hours free parking. If anyone were to stay in the cark park for longer than the 2 hours, they would be charged £12.50 per hour. Sally came back to her car at 19:00pm. How much money does she owe the car park?

Answer [   ]

5. James and Sarah went on their honeymoon to Antigua for 7 weeks. How many days does this mean they were abroad for?

Answer [   ]

6. The hairdressers charge £20 per haircut for gents and £40 per cut for ladies. In one day they had 8 clients in the salon. 6 of the clients were men and the other 2 were women. How much money did they take?

Answer [   ]

7. The lady owned 5 cats. She buys pouches of cat food every week for the cats at 80p each. She needs a pouch a day for each cat. How much does she spend per week on cat food?

Answer [   ]

8. A dance company had 1,000 dancers performing in one particular night. 35% of those dancers were sick that night and could not perform. How many dancers were left to perform in the show?

Answer [   ]

9. A car accident took place at 8:00pm on Wednesday night. The road was shut for 1 day and 3 hours. What time did the road open?

Answer [   ]

10. Tommy had 12 apples and 3 people to share them amongst. The ratio he had to share them out was 4:3:5. How many did they get each?

Answer [   ]

11. A company employed 24,000 people in one particular year. What was the average per month?

Answer [   ]

12. Sally had 1,800 red balls and Tom had 1,500. If they put all the balls together and then divided them equally between the two, how many balls would they get each?

Answer [   ]

13. Tom and Sarah went away on holiday for 5 weeks. How many days in total did they go away for?

Answer [   ]

14. Sandy drew 4 squares and 6 rectangles on a piece of paper. How many of those angles were 90 degrees?

Answer [   ]

15. Mandy has 3 dogs. She buys dog food every two weeks. She needs 1 tin of dog food per day, per dog. Each tin costs £1.20. How much does Mandy spend every two weeks on dog food?

Answer [   ]

16. David parked his car in a car park at 7:00 pm. The car park charges £5.50 per hour after 7:00 pm. David got back to his car at 11:00pm. How much does David have to pay?

Answer [   ]

17. Lucy bought 3 apples, 2 bananas and an orange. Each apple costs 55p, each banana costs 65p and each orange is 60p each. Lucy pays with a £10 note. How much change will she receive?

Answer

18. A salon charges £12.50 for gentleman's cuts and £25.00 for ladies cuts. One particular day the salon had 9 clients, 5 of which were male. How much money did the salon make that day?

Answer

19. A football stadium holds 45,000 spectators. 65% of the spectators were male. How many spectators were men?

Answer

20. A concert was expecting 26,000 people that night. The ratio of police needed for the concert would be 1:130 people. How many police would be needed for that night?

Answer

21. A child had £5.00 to spend in a sweet shop. She picked up a bag of crisps costing £1.20, a bottle of pop costing £0.60 and a bag of sweets costing £2.10. How much change would she receive?

Answer

22. Sam drew 5 equilateral triangles on a page. How many angles were 60 degrees?

Answer [   ]

23. An accident on the motorway occurred at 1300 hours. It took 5 hours for the police to open up the road. What time was traffic able to move again?

Answer [   ]

24. Heavy rain during the week resulted in the bridge being closed between the hours of 1445 and 1630 on Tuesday, 1125 and 1350 on Wednesday and 0700 and 1115 on Thursday. For how long (in hours and minutes) was the bridge closed altogether?

Answer [   ]

25. Mia and Richard went on holiday from January 1st to March 22nd. How many days did Mia and Richard have on holiday in total? (Count from the first day they left to the last day they were there.)

[   ]
Answer

ANSWERS TO NUMBERS EXERCISE 3

1. 200

2. 6 hours 45 minutes

3. 28

4. £50

5. 49

6. £200

7. £28.00

8. 650

9. Thursday night, 11pm

10. 4:3:5

11. 2,000 per month

12. 1,650

13. 35

14. 40

15. £50.40

16. £22.00

17. £6.45

18. £162.50

19. 29,250 male spectators

20. 200 police needed

21. £1.10

22. 15

23. 1800

24. 8hrs and 25minutes

25. 81 days

NUMBERS EXERCISE 4

NUMBERS EXERCISE 4

Try to answer the questions quickly and without the use of a calculator. You have 12 minutes in which to answer the 25 questions.

1. Tommy carried out his weekly food shop, which came to £178.00 in total. If he used a 20% discount voucher at checkout, how much would he pay?

Answer

2. Jane wants to buy a dress that costs £20.00. If it was discounted by 15%, how much would Jane have to pay for the dress?

Answer

3. Michael paid £45.00 for 4 films. On average how much did he pay for each film?

Answer

4. A singing choir consists of 72 people. The male to female ratio of the choir is 2:6. How many people are male in the choir?

Answer

5. Elliott drew 12 squares and 3 rectangles on the computer. How many right angles are there?

Answer

6. A company employed 28,000 people in one particular year but they had to let go 25% of their employees. How many people did they have to let go?

Answer [   ]

7. Rachel wanted to buy a top costing £17.50, a pair of trousers costing £12.50 and a jumper costing £9.00. Rachel would receive a 10% discount of the final cost. How much would Rachel have to pay?

Answer [   ]

8. A school play had an audience of 150 people. The ratio of grandparents to parents is 2:3. How many grandparents and how many parents were at the school play?

Answer [   ]

9. Peter buys 5 films costing £6.00 each and 3 books that cost £4.60 each. How much did Peter spend altogether?

Answer [   ]

10. A cruise ship would take 32 hours to reach its final destination. If the ship leaves on Monday at 1300 hours, what day would the ship arrive at its final destination?

Answer [   ]

11. Heavy snow during the week resulted in a countryside road being closed between the hours of 0845 and 1430 on Tuesday, 1125 and 1650 on Wednesday and 1600 and 2315 on Friday. For how long (in hours and minutes) was the bridge closed altogether?

Answer [   ]

12. A company employed 3,550 people in one particular year and 30% of staff received a bonus at the end of the year. How many employees received a bonus?

Answer [   ]

13. Tommy had 32 sweets. He had to share them equally between himself and 3 other people. How many sweets did they each receive?

Answer [   ]

14. Gareth had 4 yellow balls, 2 pink balls and 1 orange ball. What is the ratio?

Answer [   ]

15. Sandra bought 5 tops costing £70.50 in total. On average, how much was each top?

Answer [   ]

16. If Sammy drew 6 triangles, altogether how many degrees are there?

Answer [   ]

17. Alana had 100 pairs of shoes. She decided to get rid of a quarter of them. How many pairs of shoes does Alana have left?

Answer [   ]

18. A lady has 2 goats and 3 pigs. The cost of a bag of goat food is £23.50

and a bag of pig food costs £17.60. In a month, she needs 3 bags of goat food and 5 bags of pig food. How much money does the lady spend per month?

Answer

19. There are 45 men and 15 women in a pub. What is the ratio, in its simplest form, of males to females?

Answer

20. Elliott has 3 times more football trophies than Brad, who has 6 football trophies. How many football trophies does Elliott have?

Answer

21. A child goes in to a shop with a £10.00 note. He spends 10% of his money. How much money does the child have left?

Answer

22. Tom receives £560 a week. On average how much does Tom get per day?

Answer

23. There are 20 cats and 5 rabbits in a pet shelter. What is the ratio, in its simplest form, of cats to rabbits?

Answer

24. Billy had 500 x 1p coins and 100 x 2p coins. How much money does Billy have altogether?

Answer [   ]

25. Lucy works 20 hours a week and she gets paid £7 per hour. How much money does Lucy earn in 4 weeks?

Answer [   ]

ANSWERS TO NUMBERS EXERCISE 4

1. £142.40

2. £17.00

3. £11.25

4. 18 male

5. 60

6. 7000 people

7. £35.10

8. 60 grandparents and 90 parents

9. £43.80

10. Tuesday 9pm

11. 18hours and 25 minutes

12. 1065 people

13. 8 sweets each

14. 4:2:1

15. £14.10

16. 1080

17. 75

18. £158.50

19. 3:1
20. 18 trophies
21. £9.00
22. £80 per day
23. 4:1
24. £7.00
25. £560

NUMBERS EXERCISE 5

Get FREE access to more tests at:

www.PsychometricTestsOnline.co.uk

NUMBERS EXERCISE 5

Try to answer the questions quickly and without the use of a calculator. You have 12 minutes in which to answer the 25 questions.

1. Polly draws 16 squares on a page. In total, how many degrees are there?

Answer

2. Melissa goes clothes shopping with £50 in her purse. How many tops could Melissa buy if each top was £8.50?

Answer

3. Joey had 150 sweets and he had to share them between himself and 5 other people. If Joey shared them equally, how many sweets would they have each?

Answer

4. A storm hit a town at approximately 2200 hours Monday night. The storm lasted for 16 hours. At what time did the storm end?

Answer

5. Rachel and two housemates went food shopping for the week. They split the cost between them. The food shopping comes to £360.60. How much does each of them have to pay?

Answer

6. Dawn goes to the pet store. She buys 2 cats, 5 goldfish and 3 guinea pigs. A cat costs £16.50, a goldfish costs 80p and a guinea pig costs £6.80. In total, how much does Dawn spend?

Answer [   ]

7. Two companies merge together. One company has 8,880 employees and the other 4,560. Between both companies, they have to let go 10% of employees. How many employees will be left?

Answer [   ]

8. Sophie has 8 times more awards than her best friend Claire. Sophie has 24. How many awards does Claire have?

Answer [   ]

9. Claire has 6 cats. She buys cat food every week. Each cat uses one tin of cat food per day. How many tins of cat food does Claire need to buy for one week?

Answer [   ]

10. A stadium holds 18,000 spectators. The ratio of police to spectators must be 1:90. How many police would be needed if the stadium was full?

Answer [   ]

11. Nathan has 40 basketball jerseys and he decides to give 25% of them to his nephew. How many jerseys is Nathan left with?

Answer [   ]

12. Sam wanted to buy the new England football kit for himself and his two

children. The kits cost £46.99 for an adult size and £16.99 for a child size. In total, how much money would Sam have to spend if he were to buy the football kit for himself and his two children?

Answer [   ]

13. Adam is the coach of a football team. He wanted to buy himself and all the team new football shirts for the next match. There are 19 football players on his team and each top would cost £17.50. If Adam receives a 20% discount on the total cost, how much would Adam have to pay?

Answer [   ]

14. A family of 4 all have jobs. Two members earn £150 a week and the other two members earn £75 a week. How much money does the whole family earn in a 4 week period?

Answer [   ]

15. Shaun has 500 marbles. He loses ¼ of them. How many marbles does Shaun have left?

Answer [   ]

16. Ella is going on holiday for two weeks. She wants to buy one swimsuit to wear for every day she is away. How many swimsuits will Ella need?

Answer [   ]

17. Four people are going on holiday. In total, the holiday costs £2,880. On average, how much money will each person have to pay?

Answer [   ]

18. Sally took 4 children to a play centre for the day. A children's pass costs £5.50 for the day. The policy of the day care is "pay for 2 children and 1 goes free". How much did it cost Sally to take her 4 children?

Answer [   ]

19. In a fish tank there are 12 white fish and 6 gold fish. What is the ratio of white to gold fish?

Answer [   ]

20. Ryan works 3 days a week and he earns £75 a day. How much money does Ryan earn if he works for 36 days?

Answer [   ]

21. Julie has 19 marbles. Her friends Justin and Tom have 36 marbles each. In total how many marbles do they have in total?

Answer [   ]

22. A library has 20,000 books on record. It is shown that each year 35% of books are not returned. How many books are not returned each year?

Answer [   ]

23. James buys a new suit. It is discounted at 20%. The suit costs £68.00. With the discount, how much does the suit cost James?

Answer [   ]

24. Andy has £10 and he decides to share his money between his 3 daughters. If Andy shares out the money equally, how much money would his 3 daughters each receive?

Answer [   ]

25. A beauty salon charges £12.50 for a half leg wax and £19.00 for a full leg wax. That day, the salon does 5 half leg waxes and 8 full leg waxes. How much money does the salon take that day?

Answer [   ]

ANSWERS TO NUMBERS EXERCISE 5

1. 5760

2. 5 tops

3. 25

4. 1400 on Tuesday

5. £120.20 each

6. £57.40

7. 12096

8. 3

9. 42 tins of cat food

10. 200

11. 30

12. £80.97

13. £280

14. £1800

15. 375

16. 14

17. £720

18. £16.50

19. 2:1

20. £2700

21. 91

22. 7000

23. £54.40

24. £3.33

25. £214.50

NUMBERS EXERCISE 6

Get FREE access to more tests at:

www.PsychometricTestsOnline.co.uk

NUMBERS EXERCISE 6

Try to answer the questions quickly and without the use of a calculator. You have 12 minutes in which to answer the 25 questions.

1. A company goes into administration and they are selling all of their stock with a 60% discount. If a coat costs £45.00 at full price, how much would it cost with the 60% discount?

Answer [   ]

2. Martin buys some new holiday clothes. He buys a top costing £14.99, two pairs of shorts for £20 and a pair of sandals costing £8.50. He pays with a £50 note. How much change does Martin get?

Answer [   ]

3. Sam went to sleep at 10:30pm and he managed to get exactly 8 and half hours sleep. What time did Sam wake up?

Answer [   ]

4. Jack has 40 magic beans. He plants ¾ of them. How many magic beans does Jack have left?

Answer [   ]

5. If a concert starts at 9:15pm and it lasts for 9 hours, what time does the concert finish?

Answer [   ]

6. January has 31 days. That month, Jane received £1,085 bonus from work. On average, how much did Jane get for each day of the month?

Answer [   ]

7. Tom finishes school at 3.15pm and he must be home by 7pm. How long does Tom have out before he has to be home?

Answer [   ]

8. A teacher has 28 English papers to mark for her class. Each paper will take 9 minutes to mark. How long in hours and minutes will the teacher spend marking the papers?

Answer [   ]

9. A father goes into a shop to buy new pairs of trainers for each of his 3 children. He has £100 to spend. If he were to equally split the money between the 3 children, what is the maximum amount he could spend on each of his children's trainers?

Answer [   ]

10. Harry goes in to a video store where each video costs £6.50. If he has £50 on his possession, how many videos can he buy?

Answer [   ]

11. A student needs to buy 5 books for their university course and they have £35.00 on their possession. If each book costs £4.50, how much money does

the student have left?

Answer [   ]

12. A grandmother goes into a shop and spends £160. How much does she have to pay if she uses her 15% discount card?

Answer [   ]

13. A museum has 60 classic items. They are giving away a ¼ of these classic items to auction. How many items do they have to give away?

Answer [   ]

14. Sarah goes to see a musical in the west end. The show lasts for 3 hours and has a 45 minute break half way through. If the show starts at 5:45pm, what time will the show finish?

Answer [   ]

15. A CD store holds up to 15,000 CD's and 15% of these are rock and roll. How many CD's are rock and roll?

Answer [   ]

16. Mia has 12 times as many cousins as her friend Sophie. If Mia has 36 cousins, how many cousins does Sophie have?

Answer [   ]

17. Michael spent £160 in one shop and £95.50 in another. How much money did Michael spend altogether?

Answer [   ]

18. A royal parade was taking place midday on Sunday. The road was shut from 2100 Saturday night and opened again at 2200 on Sunday night. How many hours was the road shut for?

Answer [   ]

19. On average, if a police officer arrested 112 people in 4 weeks, how many people did he arrest a day?

Answer [   ]

20. The ambulance service received a call at 1300 hours. Due to a traffic jam, it took them 150 minutes to reach the scene. What time did they arrive at the scene?

Answer [   ]

21. A pregnant woman was expecting her baby on the 1st May. The baby arrived 18 days early. What date was the baby born?

Answer [   ]

22. If a concert ticket costs £25.60 and a group of 11 people went, how much in total would the group spend on tickets?

Answer [   ]

23. A family goes through a carton of milk a day. A carton of milk costs £1.55. If the family were to buy their milk for the next 8 days, how much would they spend?

Answer

24. A family of four went to a restaurant for dinner. Each course was £7.50 and each person had two courses in total. How much did the entire meal cost?

Answer

25. A family of 6 split the cost of all the household bills. The water bill was £70.80, the gas bill was £20.00 and the electric bill was £35.00, the rent for the month is £540. How much does each member of the family put towards covering the bill costs?

Answer

ANSWERS TO NUMBERS EXERCISE 6

1. £18.00

2. £6.51

3. 7:00am

4. 10

5. 6:15am

6. £35

7. 3 hours and 45 minutes

8. 4 hours and 12 minutes

9. £33.33

10. 7

11. £12.50

12. £136

13. 15

14. 9:30pm

15. 2250

16. 3

17. £255.50

18. 25 hours

19. 4 people a day

20. 1530

21. 13th of April

22. £281.60

23. £12.40

24. £60

25. £110.97

NUMBERS EXERCISE 7

Get FREE access to more tests at:

www.PsychometricTestsOnline.co.uk

NUMBERS EXERCISE 7

Try to answer the questions quickly and without the use of a calculator. You have 25 minutes in which to answer the 25 questions.

1. A cruise ship has 13 rows of windows. If each row has 39 windows, how many windows are there in total?

a.498

b.507

c.527

d.618

e.627

Answer [   ]

2. In a car park there are 325 cars, and each car has 4 tyres and 1 spare tyre. How many tyres are there throughout the car park?

a.1,525

b.1,575

c.1,650

d.1,675

e.1,625

Answer [   ]

3. A greengrocer has a box of 360 strawberries. The greengrocer wants to make up punnets of strawberries, each with 36 strawberries in it. How many punnets of strawberries can the greengrocer make?

a.6

b.10

c.12

d.26

e.36

Answer [   ]

4. A ball of wool measures 3.3 metres. If you have 100 balls of wool, how many metres will there be?

a.3.30 metres

b.33.0 metres

c.330 metres

d.3,300 metres

e.660 metres

Answer [   ]

5. How many pieces of string measuring 1.25 metres in length can be cut from a ball which is 100m long?

a.12.5

b.125

c.80

d.250

e.100

Answer [   ]

6. One case containing 42 cartons of orange juice costs £6.30. How much will two cartons of orange juice cost?

a.10p

b.15p

c.25p

d.30p

e.45p

Answer [   ]

7. A moped is travelling at a speed of 35 mph. How long does it take to travel 7 miles?

a.6 minutes

b.10 minutes

c.24 minutes

d.8 minutes

e.12 minutes

Answer [   ]

8. A train travels a total distance of 540 miles at a constant speed of 90 mph. How long does the journey last?

a.360 minutes

b.320 minutes

c.240 minutes

d.300 minutes

Answer [   ]

9. What speed do you need to travel to go 100 miles in 2 hours?

a.25 mph

b.200 mph

c.10 mph

d.20 mph

e.50 mph

Answer [   ]

10. A prisoner has escaped from prison. The prison is 20 miles away. You need to get there in 15 minutes. How fast do you need to drive?

a.40 mph

b.60 mph

c.80 mph

d.85 mph

e.90 mph

Answer [   ]

11. A CD album has 49 minutes worth of songs. If each song is 3 minutes 30 seconds long, how many songs are on the album?

a.7

b.14

c.15

d.28

e.18

Answer [   ]

12. A coach driver is making a journey form Land's End to John O'Groats. This is a distance of 420 miles. He has to make 7 equal stops. How many miles apart does each stop have to be?

a.60

b.80

c.45

d.70

e.50

Answer [   ]

13. A train has 6 trams and each tram holds 80 tonnes of freight. What is the total weight of freight carried by the train?

a.380 tonnes

b.420 tonnes

c.480 tonnes

d.570 tonnes

e.580 tonnes

Answer [   ]

14. An office has 333 computer desks. If only 2/3 are used, how many are un-used?

a.33

b.90

c.111

d.222

e.22

Answer [   ]

15. Mike cycles every day for 30 minutes. How much time does he spend cycling over 8 days?

a.3.5 hours

b.4 hours

c.4.5 hours

d.5 hours

e.5.5 hours

Answer [   ]

16. A rugby club raises its annual subscription of £300 by 25%. What will the new subscription be?

a.£345

b.£360

c.£370

d.£375

e.£385

Answer [   ]

17. A cinema ticket costs £5.00. If a pensioner is given a 15% discount, how much change will they get from a £20 note?

a.£15.25

b.£15.45

c.£15.75

d.£16.25

e.£16.30

Answer [   ]

18. A circle has a diameter of 240 mm. What is the length, in centimetres, of the radius?

a.12 cm

b.18 cm

c.22 cm

d.6 cm

e.24 cm

Answer [   ]

19. Below is a bar chart showing yearly vegetable sales for a market in Castleton. What is the average yearly sale of mushrooms over the three years?

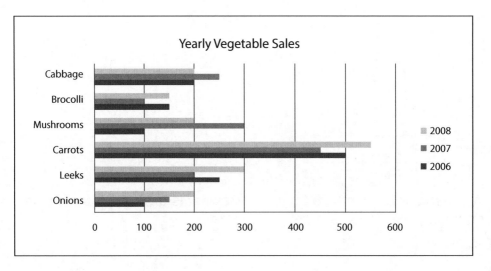

a.200

b.225

c.250

d.300

e.350

Answer [   ]

20. Roger needs to lay new turf in his garden. The whole of the garden will need new turf. Calculate the area of the garden that will need new turf.

a.66 ft²

b.112 ft²

c.128 ft²

d.132 ft²

e.144 ft²

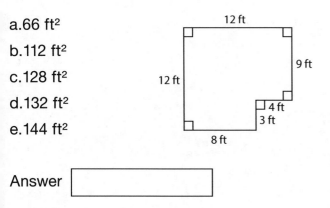

Answer [   ]

21. If I have £40 in my wallet and spend £13.75 of it, how much will I have left?

a.£25.75

b.£26.25

c.£27.50

d.£28.15

e.£29.60

Answer [   ]

22. A motorist is travelling at 80mph. How far will he have travelled in 15 minutes?

a.10 miles

b.15 miles

c.12 miles

d.25 miles

e.20 miles

Answer [   ]

23. A prison cell holds two people. There are two prison areas: high risk and low risk. The high risk area has 123 cells and the low risk area has 334 cells.

How many prisoners are there in the prison?

a.897

b.910

c.914

d.1,010

e.1,028

Answer [   ]

24. A food processing company has 10 people a week absent due to illness. How many people are absent due to illness in a year?

a.520

b.730

c.1,040

d.3,640

e.3,650

Answer [   ]

25. Balmoray Police operates a three-shift working pattern in each day. Each shift has to have 22 police officers on duty. How many officers are required for a days work?

a.66

b.62

c.60

d.86

e.132

Answer [   ]

ANSWERS TO NUMBERS EXERCISE 7

1. B
2. E
3. B
4. C
5. C
6. D
7. E
8. A
9. E
10. C
11. B
12. A
13. C
14. C
15. B
16. D
17. C
18. A
19. A
20. D
21. B
22. E
23. C
24. A
25. A

NUMBERS EXERCISE 8

Get FREE access to more tests at:

www.PsychometricTestsOnline.co.uk

NUMBERS EXERCISE 8

1. In the Johnson family there are 7 people; 3 of them are female. What is this as a fraction?

a.2/3

b.4/6

c.3/7

d.6/15

e.1/3

Answer [   ]

2. You are at a traffic collision in Glasgow where a vehicle has crashed into a play area. As part of your documentation you need to calculate the area of the playing field. Using the diagram below, work out the area of the playing field and select the appropriate answer.

a.700 m²

b.900 m²

c.1,200 m²

d.1,300 m²

e.1,400 m²

Answer [   ]

3. Your yearly salary is £40,000. You also receive a yearly bonus which is 15% of your salary. How much do you earn per year?

a.£40,060

b.£40,600

c.£46,000

d.£49,000

e.£56,000

Answer [ ]

4. On a housing estate in Edinburgh there are 34,000 homes. Of these homes 63% are semi-detached, 30% are detached, and the remainder are terraced houses. How many houses are terraced?

a.23.8

b.238

c.2,380

d.2,680

e.23,800

Answer [ ]

5. You have two foot patrols a day. The total distance walked is 20 miles. If you walked an average speed of 4 mph, how long is each patrol?

a.5 hours

b.3 hours 30 minutes

c.4 hours

d.2 hours 30 minutes

e.4 hours 20 minutes

Answer [ ]

6. You are tasked to drive your boss to a meeting 100 miles away. You will be driving at 60 mph. If you set off at 10:20pm, what time would you arrive?

a.11:40pm

b.12:00pm

c.12:40pm

d.12:20pm

e.12:30pm

Answer [   ]

7. A criminal sprints at a speed of 10 metres every 2 seconds (10m/ 2 seconds). How long does it take him to run 1,000 metres if he continues at the same speed?

a.100 seconds

b.10 seconds

c.200 seconds

d.20 seconds

e.25 seconds

Answer [   ]

8. You are at a fruit and vegetable stall at a market. If one apple costs 41p, how much would it cost to buy 11 apples?

a.£4.41

b.£4.21

c.£4.61

d.£4.67

e.£4.51

Answer [   ]

9. A car garage orders four new sport cars costing £41,000 each. How much in total has the garage spent on the new sports cars?

a.£124,000

b.£154,000

c.£164,000

d.£166,000

e.£168,000

Answer

10. A water tank has a maximum capacity of 200 litres. If the tank is 80% full, how many more litres are required to fill it to its maximum?

a.25 litres

b.40 litres

c.50 litres

d.55 litres

e.60 litres

Answer

11. If I spend £1.60, £2.35, £3.55 and £4.75 on a selection of goods, how much will I have spent in total?

a.£10.65

b.£11.60

c.£11.55

d.£12.25

e.£12.55

Answer

12. Below is a chart showing snowfall across the Lincolnshire region in 2004 in centimetres. What is the combined snowfall for January and May?

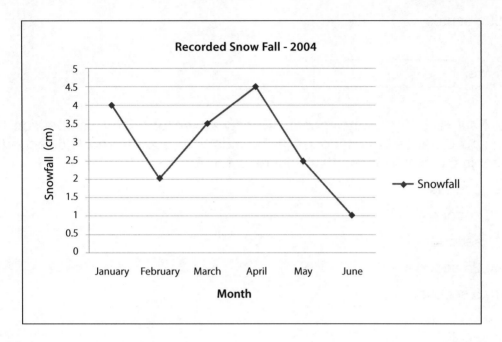

a.5.5 cm

b.6.0 cm

c.6.5 cm

d.7.0 cm

e.8.5 cm

Answer [   ]

13. On Monday it takes Lucy 52 minutes to get to work. On Tuesday it takes 40 minutes, Wednesday takes 51 minutes, on Thursday it takes 1 hour 2 minutes and on Friday it takes 1 hour 30 minutes. How long did her average commute take?

a.58 minutes

b.62 minutes

c.60 minutes

d.61 minutes

e.59 minutes

Answer [   ]

14. Paul is a 100 metre sprinter. During a weekend-long competition he runs the distance in 11 seconds, 9 seconds, 9.5 seconds and 11.5 seconds. What is the average time that Paul runs 100 metres in?

a.9 seconds

b.10 seconds

c.11 seconds

d.10.25 seconds

e.10.5 seconds

Answer [   ]

15. One in fourteen people become a victim of car crime each year. In Saxby there are 224 people. On that basis, how many people per year experience car crime in Saxby?

a.14

b.16

c.18

d.20

e.22

Answer [   ]

16. Lisa's weekly newspaper bill is £5.50 and the delivery charge is 35p per week. How much does she have to pay over six weeks?

a.£28.10

b.£31.10

c.£35.10

d.£35.20

e.£36.10

Answer [   ]

17. A gardener wants to gravel over the area shown below. One bag of gravel will cover 20 m². How many bags are needed to cover the entire garden?

a.40

b.55

c.65

d.75

e.130

10 m

50 m

40 m

20 m

Answer [   ]

18. The gardener decides he is only going to gravel 20% of the garden. Using the above diagram, how many square metres will he be gravelling?

a.26 m²

b.300 m²

c.130 m²

d.240 m²

e.260 m²

Answer [   ]

19. You stop and search 40 people, and 8 of them are arrested for possession of a class A drug. What is this as a fraction?

a.1/3

b.1/4

c.1/6

d.1/10

e.1/5

Answer [   ]

20. There are 144 people entered into a raffle, 12 people each win a prize.
What is this as a fraction?

a.1/6

b.1/8

c.1/12

d.1/24

e.1/10

Answer [   ]

21. At a music festival there are 35,000 festival goers, 5% of these are under
16 years of age. How many festival goers were under 16?

a.1500

b.1750

c.2500

d.3500

e.7000

Answer [   ]

22. At Christmas you buy 30 presents; 12 are bought for your family and 18 for your friends. What percentage was bought for your friends?

a.20%

b.30%

c.40%

d.60%

e.75%

Answer [   ]

23. Over one year, PC Smith files details of 600 drink driving cases. These are divided into 5 piles dependant upon how over the limit the drink driver was. If the piles are all equal sizes, how many are in each pile?

a.115 files

b.120 files

c.125 files

d.130 files

e.135 files

Answer [   ]

24. On average, 1 out of every 30 people experience back problems in their lifetime. Out of 900 people, how many will experience back problems?

a.20

b.30

c.60

d.90

e.120

Answer [   ]

25. Below are a toy company's monthly sale figures. Calculate the average toy sales per month for the year.

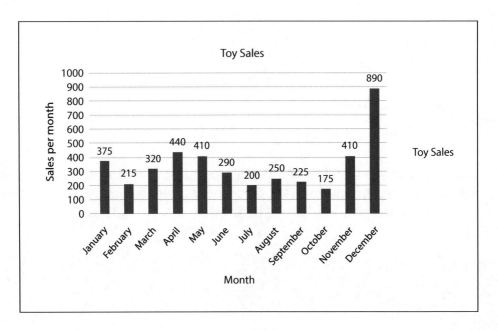

a.350

b.375

c.450

d.500

e.700

Answer [   ]

ANSWERS TO NUMBERS EXERCISE 8

1. C

2. B

3. C

4. C

5. D

6. B

7. C

8. E

9. C

10. B

11. D

12. C

13. E

14. D

15. B

16. C

17. D

18. B

19. E

20. C

21. B

22. D

23. B

24. B

25. A

A FEW FINAL WORDS

You have now reached the end of the testing guide and no doubt you will be ready to take the numbers test element of the Scottish Police Test.

The majority of candidates who pass the police officer selection process have a number of common attributes. These are as follows:

1. They believe in themselves.

The first factor is self-belief. Regardless of what anyone tells you, you can become a police officer. Just like any job of this nature, you have to be prepared to work hard in order to be successful. Make sure you have the self-belief to pass the selection process and fill your mind with positive thoughts.

2. They prepare fully.

The second factor is preparation. Those people who achieve in life prepare fully for every eventuality and that is what you must do when you apply to become a police officer. Work very hard and especially concentrate on your weak areas.

3. They persevere.

Perseverance is a fantastic word. Everybody comes across obstacles or setbacks in their life, but it is what you do about those setbacks that is important. If you fail at something, then ask yourself 'why' you have failed. This will allow you to improve for next time and if you keep improving and trying, success will eventually follow. Apply this same method of thinking when you apply to become a police officer.

4. They are self-motivated.

How much do you want this job? Do you want it, or do you *really* want it?

When you apply to join the police you should want it more than anything in the world. Your levels of self-motivation will shine through on your application and during your interview. For the weeks and months leading up to the police officer selection process, be motivated as best you can and always keep your fitness levels up as this will serve to increase your levels of motivation.

Work hard, stay focused and be what you want…

The How2become Team

P.S. Don't forget, you can get FREE access to more tests online at:

www.PsychometricTestsOnline.co.uk

NEED A LITTLE EXTRA

PASS YOUR SCOTTISH POLICE ASSESSMENTS

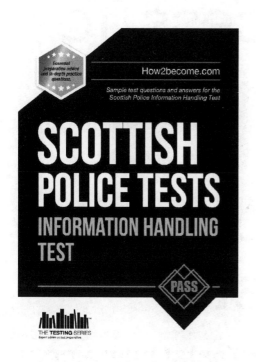

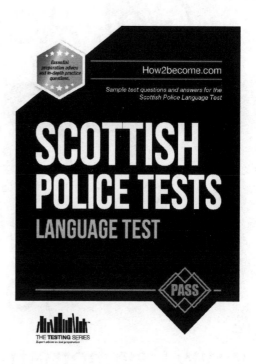

FOR MORE INFORMATION ON OUR SCOTTISH POLICE GUIDES, PLEASE VISIT

WWW.HOW2BECOME.COM

Get Access To
FREE
Psychometric Tests

www.PsychometricTestsOnline.co.uk

Attend a 1 Day Police Officer Training Course at:

www.PoliceCourse.co.uk